TEN POETS
Vol.2

James Domestic

Mary Dickins

Barry King

Lorna Mackinnon

Stuart Webb

E.D. Evans

Sam Marsh

Darren J Beaney

David Chidgey

Lea Marie

Published by Earth Island Books

Pickforde Lodge

Pickforde Lane

Ticehurst

East Sussex

TN5 7BN

www.earthislandbooks.com

ISBN 9781916864481

Printed and bound by Solopress, Southend

Contents

JAMES DOMESTIC

James grew up in Essex, is a poet, songwriter, musician, DJ, painter, and punk. Currently, he has three illustrated volumes of poetry – 'Domesticated' Vols.1 to 3 – published by Earth Island Books, another, co-authored collection ('Cruor', with Dave Cullern), and a chapbook, ('Amateurcrastinator') published by Backroom Poetry. He has appeared on BBC Breakfast telly and numerous radio shows and podcasts.

His work has been praised by poets and punks alike, including Mark Grist, Steve Ignorant, Dick Lucas, Jerry A., Scott Coe, Attila The Stockbroker, and The Shend. He currently resides in Suffolk.

www.earthislandbooks.com

www.jamesdomestic.com

For live bookings email jamesdomestic@hotmail.com

STEAK

Just once, would it kill you?
A little recognition?
Tight-lipped as ever
Give nothing away; not a crumb

"Too much praise makes kids weak"
I've heard you say it in the pub garden
And at home too, at the dinner table
But I'm bloody starving here
Just look at me: emotionally emaciated

Can't bring yourself to offer a morsel
You give more to the ducks in the park!
And I've done so much more
to try to earn your favour
than those bloody ducks
So much more

But the less you give
The harder I try
And I don't know if you even notice
Filled to the brim with aggregates as you are

My efforts unheeded
Not a single point awarded

for any of my performances

Acknowledgement zero

Days, weeks, months, and years

Every mission thwarted by indifference

And still I go on, trying my hardest

Hurling my bloodied soul against the wall

just to see if it'll stick

Too stubborn, or too stupid to let it rest

To let it die

A thousand times or more

I've given you my best

I just want you to say to me

what you say to the waiter

when he asks

how you like your steak

RACIST NAN

She's a funny ol' girl
There's no mistaking it
If she spies an empty gob
then she'll stuff some cake in it
Topping up your tea
like an empty cup's a sin
With an intravenous drip
she couldn't get more in

Insists on giving you money
every time that you go round
'cos you changed a bulb, or brought some milk
now that she's housebound
A scrunched up fiver in your hand
and a pink lipsticky peck
She thinks her TV's remote control
is needlessly hi-tech

She's always been so good to you
but lately things are strained
She says things that are racist
then laughs like a fucking drain
You find you're visiting less and less
as you find her views so gross
You feel guilty if you pop in

and much the same if you don't

Many times you've tried to bridge
these chasms of conversation
Try to understand her point of view
and counter them with patience
But you can't be there as often
as the daily Daily Mail
Whose ideologies she parrots
every visit without fail

You drop in one day after work
and things come to a head
You know you've been fighting a losing battle
when this is what she says:
"*I know that you don't like it*
That your nan's views are racist
But they are and always will be
I'm old fashioned, and you hate it"
She must see my deflation
If not my broken heart
"*Yeah, you're nan's a bloody racist*
HA! HA! HA!"

Next year she takes the kind of trip
the old take only once
A nose-dive halfway down the stairs

Neighbours call an ambulance

And sat beside her on the ward

with her bruises, breaks and tubes

Eyes moist from my sadness

and from our grievance too

Our bond soured by her bigotry

and that she thought it such a lark

My nan, the racist

HA! HA! HA!

PLEASE DON'T DROP IN OVER CHRISTMAS

You instigate
vaginal dryness
You think you're a plus
But you're really a minus

You regularly cause
erectile dysfunction
You'd end it all
But you ain't got the gumption

You prompt outbreaks
of postulant boils
You're greasy and dirty
Like my nan's chip pan oil

When you enter a kitchen
you curdle the cream
You've got body odour
And your breath is extreme

You're a nasty piece of work
by anyone's estimate
Heartless and cruel
You're proper Old Testament

You make the enamel
melt from all teeth
We chipped in for flowers
It was a wreath

You infect all you meet
With acute paranoia
Your tales are as tall
as a giant sequoia

Arranged your lank hair
in a full-on comb over
Your fetid stench
would knock a rhino over

You can't take a hint
you just can't get a clue
My politeness has withered
now I'm just gonna be rude

You're full of wind
and the solid stuff too
please don't come over
I don't want you to

No, really.
I don't want you to.

EMPLOYING AN OCTOPUS

Please do not employ an octopus
to wash up your dishes
It'd be four times quicker
but makes his tentacles itchy

Please do not berate the octopus
or cause him an affront
Don't forget:
He could strangle you
like four blokes at once

RING

Nestling in the box
Velvet-lined
I used to be taken out
and allowed to shine

I'd glint in the lights
and I'd generate awe
But I can't muster the lustre
for that anymore

I'm no longer precious
My surface has dulled
My marriage to the wearer
has now been annulled

I'm out of luck, and out of style
Disgraced and out of place
I was stolen in the early hours
and switched for worthless paste

DOG 'N' DUCK MUSIC

I don't want to go and see
Some band that's playing close to me
I've never heard of 'em before
They might be crap, so I'll ignore
'em 'til they're playing Wembley Stadium
Until then I'll just evade 'em
Six quid at The Dog 'N' Duck?
D'ya take me for some kinda shmuck?

A five minute walk, up by the square
If they're good, why are they playin' there?
Are they on the front of magazines?
Do they play 'em on the BBC?
Has Jools Holland had 'em on?
No? That's where they're going wrong!
Have they been on Sunday Brunch?
No? My God! What a useless bunch!

I won't go out on a cultural limb
I just wouldn't know where to begin
I need a blitz of information
Coverage and plaudits on every station

Then I may lend them an ear

And celebrity fans would make things clear

A mainstream green light must be supplied

Populism is my guide

I'll decide I like 'em too

When lots of others say they do

And if they get big by some stroke of luck

I'll claim I saw 'em in The Dog 'N' Duck

MONUMENT

Catch a glimpse of myself

in the department store mirror

I can see my bodywork

and my interior

Scratched

Dented

Worn thin

Virtually scrap

A juicy pear

Briefly ripe with promise

But the eatin' window was missed

And now it's home to a weevil

Or many weevils

It's hard to tell exactly

But it ain't tasty; I'll tell you that much

It's mush

Eaten from the inside

Caved in

The decline rips through

like a forest fire

No sweet, only sour now

Puckered like an arsehole

Lemon juice blood

A vinegar enema swirls through and around

Disappointment marrow-deep

Salted ventricles

like gritted roads

(to match the teeth)

Aggrieved

Hazardous

Partially redacted for the sake of us all

Valleys around the eyes

A dozen Grand Canyons

Plenty lost in there

Donkeys

Dreams

All sorts

Best not look too close or you won't sleep tonight

Fingernails ragged

Nerves too

Not scared of death

Nor willing it on

Medication flat line

No mountains and no chasms

Just a levelled spirit

A satin magnolia finish

for the soul

On and on and on and on

I thought I knew it all
and blundered into living
at a speed I could not maintain
Impatient to make things happen
I mistook appetite for hunger
and gorged without care
Haste for haste's sake
And to what end?

I couldn't keep my powder dry
or rest for a single beat
And now I am a crumbling monument
to regret

MARY DICKINS

Mary has been on television and radio as part of the Nationwide Building Society poetry ad campaign and has dished up poems all over the country as part of the Poetry Takeaway team.

Her debut, *Happiness FM* was published in 2020 and was selected by the NHS as one of 10 uplifting books for the NHS and has been made available in every NHS library. In 2022 Mary was featured in The Guardian regarding her experience of coming to performance poetry later in life. Her latest collection is *Late Shift at the Pickle Factory* (Burning Eye, 2023).

happinessfm.bigcartel.com

marydickins.wixsite.com/pragmaticpoet

Instagram: @marydickins

DAWN CHORUS

I should get up to greet the dawn
to bathe myself in early light
I could become transformed reborn
I should get up to greet the dawn
to frolic on the dew-soaked lawn
when all is bountiful and bright
I should get up to greet the dawn
and rid myself of doubt and scorn

I should get up to greet the dawn
escape the dark embrace of night
I must not simply stretch and yawn
I must get up to greet the dawn
I must not lie here wracked and torn
and blame my torpor for my plight
I must get up to greet the dawn
when all is bountiful and bright

I will get up to greet the dawn
tomorrow I will do it all
take note that I have solemnly sworn
I will get up to greet the dawn
right now my bed's too snug and warm
to answer that celestial call
I will get up to greet the dawn
tomorrow I will do it all

POEM IN WHICH SHE BRIEFLY CONSIDERED BOTOX

her face was like a room in need of refurbishment
as if through a window she noted history writing
itself on her skin and this was the thought
that struck her silent in the face of the commotion
that followed as she foresaw herself hauled to an
early reckoning her pretensions just so much stuff
given the decline of her ectodermal tissue yet still
she wished so much and in the face of such
dilapidation she perished the thought of surrender
yearning to claw back that which those sneak thief
years had taken from her but this was not the place
or the time to begrudge her sleeker sisters
or to mourn and wail about this and that so she
let go accepted she would no longer floor people
with her dazzle rather she would wait
and watch life carve its furrows and creases
again and again and just as the familiar swam
back into focus her brief yearning for youth
was simply forgotten and she continued afterwards
much as before the thought occurred to her

THINGS ARE NOT ALWAYS WHAT THEY SEEM

A Cumulonimbus won't always bring rain.
It threatens then passes as fast as it came.
A sequence of notes isn't always a tune.
A small mound of sand isn't strictly a dune.
People who proselytize god are still sinners.
Those who get prizes are not always winners.
Things that are borrowed haven't always been lent.
An honest visage doesn't mean you're not bent.
Being well-read doesn't mean you are versed.
A heartfelt rendition isn't always rehearsed.
A roof and four walls isn't always a home.
Solitary isn't the same as alone.

Catastrophes happen and no one's to blame.
A Cumulonimbus won't always bring rain.

DAVOS

shindig where big wigs pit wits in the sticks

and big hitters fix tricks while telling glib fibs

at glittery soirees and holding elite binges

meanwhile this ship is sinking lickety-split

but billionaires still maintain dominion

and the skint get slim pickings on the brink

of extinction as these sick slick- witted gits

rip off minions and rig it so despite economic

blips skinflint profiteers will still be rich

INSTRUCTIONS FOR A FUNERAL

On waking forget this is the day
then in a cold sweat remember.

Wear black if that is the expectation.
Select a cheerful scarf for a colourful life.

Choose stout shoes for a muddy graveyard.
Peer through the window at grey sleet.

Pack tissues and a hip flask of brandy.
Gather at the house if requested.

Gasp as the hearse glides to a halt.
The coffin will seem too small for its occupant.

Choke down a clod of sadness.
Climb into a waiting car.
Wonder how many will gather for you?

Repair your mascara.
Alight and crunch across the gravel.
Embrace frail family through flimsy garments.
Nod sagely at the eulogies
and privately word your own.
Sing and hear your voice high pitched and discordant.

Shudder as the coffin glides silently into the abyss.
Pocket the order of service as a crumpled keepsake.

Later at whatever functions as a wake
drink cheap wine
and laugh inappropriately turning heads.

Consume triangular sandwiches, brittle chicken wings
and some cold dead pork pie. Move on to gin.

Disconcert elderly relatives
by the telling of loud anecdotes
then chain smoke enthusiastically
with fellow mourners

huddled in bleak bonhomie by the exit.
Thank your hosts profusely.
Promise to come by knowing you won't.
Return to your city that has not missed a beat.
At home weep until your head feels hollow.
Mostly for yourself.

Funerals are for the living.
Sleep. Wake up and think for a moment
there is a funeral to go to. Remember.
Then forget to remember.

STARFISH

I pose no threat I do no harm.

I sprout new selves from severed arms.

A stellate blob that doesn't shine.

My arms are eyes, my blood is brine.

No brain with which to give a damn.

I cannot think but yet I am.

FORGETFULNESS

(After Billy whatshisname)

The thingamajig is the first to go

followed by the whatchamacallit and the doodah.

Like when you can't remember

where you put the oojamaflip

and then you forget why you were looking.

It will come to me in a minute that thing

I want to say to that poet Billy something – you know

the New York one - it's on the tip of my tongue.

It seemed so important yesterday

but now I've forgotten why.

Oh yes! Perhaps I don't need to recall

the name of that flower

that I buy every Christmas

and have to google annually

because by November

its name slipped my mind again.

I don't need to remember how many litres in a gallon

or the names of the planets in descending order.

These days there's an app for everything.

Better to surrender to the shrivelling hippocampus

and the overwrought neural pathways

and just let the proper nouns glide into the ether

leaving only their essence and outline as reminders?

My plan is to tackle Sudokus

whilst fumbling for lost keys,

lost theorems and the names of symphonies.

And I'm hoping that the search engine I call brain

will continue to wake me

in the middle of the night yelling

………………COLLINS!!"

Even if I can't remember why it is I needed to know.

ON SYMI

I was thinking night thoughts,
my mind fogged like the mist we sailed through
into Saturday.
Sighing as my soul arrived.
Even the birds fly more slowly here.

I was taking photographs without a camera,
capturing absolutely the sun bearing down
on olive branches
and the chickens pacing inelegantly by the fence.

I was searching for Turkish galleys on the taut horizon.
I heard the thud of phantom jack boots
in the cobbled square.
I saw an evil eye wink from a Jesus altar.

I was yielding to the blood, flesh and sinew
of womankind.
My eyes- rheumy-with tears, my womb parched
and shrivelled
like an old fig left too long in the sun.

I was forging pathways. Finding my own patterns,
leaving small avalanches and the whiff of oregano
in my wake.

I was piling these words on top of one another
like the stones.

LAPSED CATHOLIC

once I was a tiny thing

amorphous

unengaged

determined by my DNA

only just been made

they twisted me   they bent me

so they could get me in

they shrank me and they smothered me

called everything a sin

but I am out of the mould now

it lies around me cracked

I screamed   I heaved   I battered

I pushed   I chipped   I hacked

YORKSHIRE PUDDING POEM

I went to write a poem but I couldn't find a thread

so I dug out a recipe for Yorkshire pud instead

as if this humble culinary task

could help me disengage

from my mounting apprehension

at the blankness of the page

my pudding it was glorious

with peaks and troughs and folds

it burst upon the taste buds like a story being told

it was crispy at the edges it was airy it was bold

it lingered on the inner eye

like Wordsworth's fields of gold

it spoke of onion gravy and Sunday afternoons

of fragrant roasts and family

and Mondays come too soon

it was lighter than a baby's breath, delicious

hot or cold

most people liked it better than this poem

so I'm told

IF I CALL MYSELF A POET

Will I get a club card or bonus air miles?
Will people waylay me with fatuous smiles?
Will I get a discount in selected stores?
When they eat in Nando's – do poets get more?
Should I keep my distance from prosaic friends
and stick to the functions that poets attend?
Is there any protective clothing I'll need
or a poet's code of practice I should probably read?
If do my best work on retirement to Devon
will dead poets reserve me a place up in heaven?

What if I'm an imposter and dreams turn to dust
and I end up disheartened remorseful and crushed
but I keep writing poetry knowing I must?
Will I still be a poet or not?
Please discuss.

BARRY KING

Barry is sometimes referred to as a "Political poet", but he personally identifies as someone who writes (usually in rhyme) about anything that inspires him, often with a touch of humour and with spoken word performance in mind, which he very much enjoys.

Barry is retired and lives in Colchester with his wife and naughty but lovable dog.

DONALD TRUMP DOESN'T LIKE THE W.H.O

Donald Trump doesn't like The WHO
For reasons that I Can't Explain;
I asked, and he said, Who Are You?
And that, he Won't Get Fooled Again.
Behind Blue Eyes, he thought it through,
Reminded me that, I'm A Boy,
And if The Kids Are Alright Too,
A Substitute, he'll soon employ.

Though I Can See for Miles, it's true,
And be Anyway Anyhow Anywhere,
Donald Trump doesn't like The WHO;
It's a Legal Matter beyond compare.
The Seeker of a brand new bill,
In a Magic Bus, has driven away,
And at 5.15, he'll make a deal,
With Boris the Spider, in the UK.

Donald Trump doesn't like The WHO,
His supple wrist is bound to crack;
He's acting deaf, dumb and blind too,
And My Generation's not Happy Jack.
See Me Feel Me Touch me Heal me,
Join Together; but in my view,
However much you think, I'm Free,
Donald Trump doesn't like The WHO.

FIT FOR WORK

A brown envelope comes through the door
It's painfully picked up off the floor
By a sad old man more dead than alive
Fit for work at sixty five

The cancer treatment was a success
He's had two weeks to convalesce
Now sickness pay will no longer arrive
Fit for work at sixty five

A morning appointment next Monday
In a Job centre plus ten miles away
He'll have to get a taxi, he can't drive
Fit for work at sixty five

They found him a job TWENTY miles away!
Packing boxes for minimum pay
Barely enough for a mouse to survive
Fit for work at sixty five

One year later, he's still there
Like a worn out motor in need of repair
But nothing that a hard days graft can't fix
Fit for work at sixty six

He's working triple shifts, week in week out

His sleep pattern's truly up the spout

Aching joints thrown into the mix

Fit for work at sixty six

This wasn't the life that he desired

And many of his friends have long retired

He's an old dog tired of learning new tricks

Fit for work at sixty six

He stayed with a firm nearly fifty years

But his pension plans ended up in tears

When the boss sold up and bought a yacht for kicks

Fit for work at sixty six

Ten years later he's past spent

But the government pension doesn't cover the rent

And a diet of Pot Noodles and Weetabix

Still at work at seventy six

The prostate cancer didn't come back

But he suffered a massive heart attack

And the medics couldn't resuscitate

Died at work, aged seventy eight

And so ends this tale of misery

This working man's obituary

From the day he was born till his final breath

The sum of his life?

Birth, school, work, death

HE'S ON IT

He's on it like water on sinking ships
Like a hand on the ball nicked into the slips
Like a kiss on Angelina Jolie's lips
He's on it like a seagull on a bag of chips
He's on it like a rat climbing up a drainpipe
Like a stray dog pouncing on a bag of tripe
Like mould on fruit that's gone overripe
Like Oswald on Kennedy, waiting to snipe
Like an angry driver with an urge to yell
In rush hour traffic FUCKIN HELL
Like a convict on a bunk in a prison cell
Quasimodo on the rope of the cathedral bell
He's on it like an actor on a West End stage
Like an Eastern European on the minimum wage
Like a sex scandal on The Sun's front page
Jimmy Saville's dirty hands on the underage
He's on it like a rash all over your skin
He's on it like a fox on a rubbish bin
Like an old alcoholic on a bottle of gin
Like an unsuspecting arse on a drawing pin
He's on it like a pisshead on a doner kebab
He's on it like a finger on a dried up scab
Like a hand on a Rolex at a smash and grab
Like a night clubber running for a taxi cab
He's on it like a cokehead on a big white line

Keith Floyd on a bottle of French red wine

Like Diana on the trail of another landmine

Like a picnic on the beach when the weather's fine

He's on it like a kitten on a ball of string

Like a wedding guest on a chicken wing

Like a wannabe singer who really can't sing

He's on the karaoke singing everything

Like an England captain on his best friend's wife

Like a psycho in a fight with a carving knife

Like a man on appeal in solitary strife

On suicide watch sent down for life

Like a fired torpedo on an enemy fleet

Like a new-born baby on a mother's teat

Like a man with diarrhoea on a toilet seat

He's on it like a lion on a piece of meat

He's on it like a spy on a document

That's marked "Top secret" by the government

Like Guy Fawkes underneath Parliament

With a highly explosive implement

He's on it like a gossip on a juicy tale

Like a seventies pop star on a young female

Like a bird in the garden on bread gone stale

Like a member of CAMRA on a pint of real ale

Like The Terra Nova on a frozen shore

Like Captain Scott on a mission to explore

Like a poet sitting down on a muddy floor

Writing accounts of the First World War

Like a thirsty man on a beer in the fridge
Like Kingdom Brunel on designing a bridge
Like a broker on a deal with Etheridge
Like Hillary climbing up a mountain ridge
He's on it like a multi-millionaire's son
At the Bullingdon club with his flies undone
Burning a fifty pound note for fun
Then shagging a pig in front of everyone
He's on it like a bard writing a sonnet
He's on it like bird shit on a shiny bonnet
Like an addict needing more he falls upon it
Like a junkie on a score
He's happy when he's on it

INSOMNIA

How is a street of houses not hice
If more than one mouse is ruled to be mice?
Why do the measurements height and weight
Respectively rhyme with white and mate?
How can an H be silent in hour?
What is the purpose of K in knowhow?
Where is the logic in peer or fear
If pear's like dare and deer's like near?

Why does a wound not have the same sound
As pound except when a clock's being wound?
How can the plural of hoof be hooves
Or hoofs when roofs can no longer be rooves?
Why have an N in damns but not grams?
How no sheeps when there can be lambs?
What is the need of an E in more?
Two Os in door yet never in law?

The GHT residing in bright
Silently present in fight, delight,
Insight and blight but not so in bite,
Mite, spite, kite, rite or stalagmite
Has kept me awake for many a night
And try as I might, with eyes shut tight,
I toss and turn in sleepless flight
Considering words like freight and sleight.

THE LAST OF THE MOHICANS (CHINGACHGOOK)

Walking through the churchyard, I saw him there,
An original man beyond compare,
An ancient eccentric with a Mohawk,
A pensioner punk, who wanted to talk.
He asked me if I cared to share a few
Roll-ups and cans of lukewarm Special Brew,
And listen to a serious matter;
So I sat with him and heard his patter.

He said he was a ted in 'fifty-six,
When Rock around the Clock was at the flicks.
He had a flick knife and during the show,
He slashed the seats at the Trocadero.
In the early sixties, he was a mod,
A pill popper, immaculately shod,
On a Lambretta, going up and down
Fighting with rockers in a seaside town.

In the late sixties, he found a guru,
And went to a commune in Kathmandu,
But it was run by a fake millionaire,
So he came back home, shaved off all his hair,
And in the process became a skinhead,
Moon-stomping with rude-boys Jamaican-bred;
Skins in the sixties, he said, were cool cats,

And only very rarely racist twats.

He was a Starman in 'seventy-two,
When Bowie finally made his breakthrough,
But when The Dark Side of The Moon appeared
His taste in music went deeper and weird.
He grew his hair longer, became a freak,
Saw Hawkwind and Genesis reach their peak;
Back in the day when they were worth seeing,
Before the Pistols came into being.

The filth, the fury, Mary seeing red;
The established sounds dying out or dead;
He adopted a chain from ear to nose,
And the declaration: anything goes.
He was a punk till around 'eighty-four
When the old-romantics became a bore
And for want of something better to do,
He found consolation in sniffing glue.

In 'eighty-seven he rapped with a mate
Before acid tripped him into a state
Of ecstasy, with new drugs to consume,
As DJs scratched and pumped up the volume.
And in that smiley state, he changed his name:
"Chingachgook", the chief of Mohican fame.
He'd reached a peak and he had it in mind

That he was unique: the last of his kind.

Brit-pop was hardly a sensation,
He felt it to be an imitation;
A ringing knell to the finality
And demise of originality.

The scene petered out like a dying flame.
Twenty years went by and no eras came.
With nothing but more of the same in sight,
He aimlessly drifted, without a light,
Up shit-creek with no paddle or canoe,
Drowning to the sound of Radio Two,
Trapped for an age in a digitised grave
Of Brit-pop, house, metal, mod, punk and rave.

And that was it; he had no more to say.
Silently, he sat as I walked away,
Leaving him staring blankly into space
Or maybe some other faraway place,
Where out of the blue, comes a sea of change
That's against the grain and feels a bit strange,
Unconventional , untraditional,
Alternative, cool, and original.

Chingachgook, the unique, the peerless one,
Looked tired and jaded by the time he was done

And all his anecdotes are written here,

Complete with glue, acid, roll-ups, strong beer

And the thoughts of a man long in the tooth,

Offering an observational truth:

DJs and bands are playing nothing new,

A watershed movement's long overdue.

LORNA MACKINNON

Lorna Mackinnon is a poet from Colchester in Essex. Her poetry has been called everything from "a poor man's pro" to "annoyingly good, actually" – both of which she's happy to take as a compliment. She has performed poetry at Brightlingsea Winterfest and Frinton Literary Festival, as well as at dedicated poetry events including Emotional Madness with Mary-Ann and Mates, Poetry At Events and Word Habit.

PLOT TWIST: I'M THE VILLAIN

I suppose I've always enjoyed the outfits:
The violet kiss of Maleficent's cloak, a crush on
the Joker's velvet, Cruella's commitment to
monochrome (with a scarlet slash or two).
Always known to have been prone to overdramatics.
If I think about it, that's a cast
dressing room I could easily belong to.

But I didn't believe I had the sharpness
in me, not really.
I lacked the genomes that design the casually cruel
I know that, now, my darling, you'd disagree.
Insist I swallow down spite and use it for fuel.

I'd want the last act to be memorable.
Let it be said I made a real mess of things –
Crafted an escape plan so unforgettable
I flooded every bridge with kerosene.

If you hold the mirror to the right light,
maybe I am your villain.
What an unpredictable little world we're living in.

THE BALLAD OF RATTLESNAKE CANYON

Let's set the scene, shall we?
1851: you, a cursed cactus-christened kid
Await the gush of the gold rush.
When your pockets had been picked clean
You, lone rider, strayed south.
Proving yourself, once again,
a fickle fair-weather friend.
It was a lonely life until they met.

You find a girl with a bloodstain bloom of a smile
Draped inside a dustbowl.
With gunpowder under her dress
She reminds you that few gentlemen suspect
Pistols beneath a petticoat.
Or the vial of rattlesnake venom
Encased around her throat.

You always were a sloppy shooter
A sidekick seemed the dream.
And, together, you hatched a plan
to live criminally free
The money came easily
Between you, you'd strip carts in cattle convoy
And she'd sell her body like the condemned.
Oh, it was a lowly life after they met.

The ink on the sheriff's poster barely dry

The pair harvested towns like carcasses.

Whisky-soaked and wild-eyed

They gambled away their vulture's prizes

One settlement to the second over

Always stealing away in darkness

It doesn't matter because the only thing

They want is one another

Until –

Now, I'm nothing more than the narrator

The bandit's ballad-creator.

I know not what happened

when the bank robbery went sour.

But I am here to warn you – this is no Pioneertown

No Hollywood set with the lights struck out.

Our tale ends with a tinhorn running his luck down

Striking a raw nerve

like he's mining for gold, after all those years.

It was one last kiss on the cheek

Chaste as a papercut

Stinging like the venom in that copper-coated vial.

When the smoke cleared, she was alone.

In the end it's every outlaw for themselves.

You, lone rider, disappeared west

Left her sentenced to death.

I hope the money was worth it.

CONCRETE ROOTS

You always were a nocturnal animal.

Most at home in the shadows

Slipping through streetlights

Silhouette summoning the ghosts

Of the boys you'd been raised alongside

To come out and play.

A chorus of whispers lost on the estate at midnight.

It wasn't a surprise when you left

Or that, in the end

Darkness aided you like a faithful friend

And cut courage between your teeth.

A new name on your tongue

Blue-sky dreams to feast upon.

Y'see –

Your skeleton had morphed into steel over the years

A raven with robotic wings

Hardening yourself against each new shellshock

Each bangbang**BANG** door knock

The threats and the insults.

All you ever wanted was to be ~ *soft* ~

Like the girls you saw on your phone screen

The ones they told you you'd never be.

You went off in search of it, eventually.

Years later

There were concrete rumours of a resurrection.

The nocturnal animal returns, daybreak in her jaws.

We weren't sure if your homecoming

Would see you in a ballgown or a box, babygirl.

But here you are, gaze full of petals

And the glint of steely spine

Still catching under your skin in the sunlight.

All you needed was to recover

Piece your body back together.

You spoke this life into existence, remember?

Abandoned the phantoms in the courtyard

To reinvent yourself.

Now, at last

You have friends who see you for your softness.

Not the whip crack of the bubblegum popped

But the magic of the moment

it reaches its full potential

A world of wonder, sugar-tinged and sweet.

You are soft scoop ice cream in the

Blur of a summer's day

Cool to churn on the inside of a cheek.

A little bit of hope can spell out

a big problem for some people.

But not you, babe.

Spit the lingering metallic taste at the base

Of the stairwell

Where they tried to shove an old name

Down your throat.

Open wide

Let the night amplify

The roar as you speak.

Remind them that even

God's most gentle creatures

Outlive the concrete.

MATCHSTICK MEN

The accidental arsonist sits opposite me.

Guzzling gasoline for breakfast

You insist

You don't need to change your diet

It has the desired

Effect.

You're at the whim of your own wildfire, kid.

I've lived long enough to understand

That burning boys

Grow into matchstick men

And carry on setting fires

Without the concept of a consequence.

It's turned my kin into kindling.

My lovers blaze from initial sparks

Trying to convince me they're not as flammable

As they undoubtedly are.

But the problem is insurmountable.

Oh, I've seen burning boys grow into matchstick men.

But haven't you noticed?

It's always the women

Sending up smoke signals as an SOS.

I was born a water baby

So I thought I'd know how to put you out.

But your firework footwork

Has me drowning in doubt.

I enquire if you've ever tried to extinguish

Yourself

You assure me nothing works –

This is just the way of your flimsy matchbox world.

Lean in to tame the flames

And spark one last cigarette between your lips.

Blow me a kiss if you wish.

Because you can change

But you won't fix it.

It's elemental,

Matchstick man

At least that's what you believe.

Me? If I were being generous

I'd tell you this destruction is a decoy

Remind you that the phoenix is a formative creature

And that the fire in your belly

Is worth a flicker of a chance.

But we've learned to keep our eyes

On the ghosts in the smoke.

It is easier, my darling

To love you when you are whole

And not choking on the aftermath of an inferno.

I'll ask you one last time:

Wipe the ashes from your gums

And show me your teeth.

TAKE ME

Take me like a joke.
Like the burst of a laugh
Unexpected in the hitch of your throat.

Take me like a thief in the night.
(But seriously, if you're a woman living alone,
Stop watching those true crime documentaries
before bedtime.)

Take me like I brought a balloon animal to
your knife fight
Because I was trying to lift the mood.
Weirdly, I never seem to get the timing right.

Take me like a vial of arsenic.
One last swill of defiance
Washed down with a Shakespearian kiss.

Take me like a breath
Like it's the most natural thing your body has left
To give.

Take me like an oath.
Swear it down into your bones until
You can discard later in the undergrowth.

Take me at my word.

If in doubt, swallow scripture with

your whole throat and

Take me to church, darling –

Take me *home*.

Take me like I'm nothing.

Take me like it means everything to you.

What's the worst that could happen?

MAYBE

I don't like to believe I'm good at this.
It smacks of chest-open hubris
A shattered ribcage like a fallen Icarus
To compliment sticky shoulder blades.
I force myself to remember
He was just a boy idolising his father
Which seems to be the most prevalent
Of man's chosen sin.

And what if, I too, am praying at the heels
Of someone I barely knew?
What chasm am I echoing through
In the hope this message reaches you?
And you force yourself to remember
I was just a girl aching for affection
Which seems to be the sharpest
Means to a distraction.

I don't like to believe I'm good at this
But I am learning not to live in the shadow
Of someone else's sadness
Biting back the blues and claiming them
As my own.
And I force you all to remember
I am just a woman studying the weather

And my mind is monsoon season
Which seems to be the quickest route
To an excuse for anything.

But...
I have learned to anchor firm
Against the rage of those storms
Gob open, greedy,
Swallow the heat of the trickster sun.
The wings aren't on my back any more
But that doesn't mean I can't
Invent a way through it.

I don't like to believe I am good at this.
But I am.
I am.

STUART WEBB

Stuart Webb is a poet and spoken word performer from Cambridge who is now living on the north Norfolk coast. His poetry combines intricate rhyme schemes and wordplay to create work that is fresh, entertaining and sharply observed.

With subject matter ranging from politics to technology, his poetry is full of wit and flair as he chronicles life in modern Britain with confidence and verve.

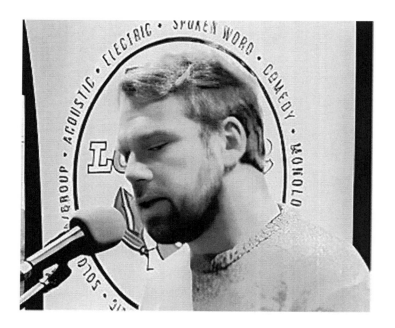

Stuart's debut chapbook of poetry 'Notes From Hysteria Island' was released in 2023 and is available through Back Room Poetry.

WE ARE LIVING IN HELL

(poetry found on GB News Facebook page)

It's finally happened. We are living in hell.

Outrageous public sector wasters

Fine parents for cheaper holidays

They choose to come here

Jean and Demon, pair of clowns

Should slim down until they're gone

Work shy Willy opens his mouth it's just

Blah blah blah

The only bollocks that springs to mind;

Is Tommy Robinson eating breakfast?

STOP THE BOATS. STOP THE WOKE.

Another leftie gobshite

Louis Walsh, Sharon Osborne

More no-go zones

This is what happens when faith is lost.

If a country believes in nothing

It's called taking the piss

Does Great Britain still exist?

NIGEL'S KAMPF

The clacking of jackboots

Up Clacton high street at dawn

Wakes him from dreams of

Great silent Zeppelins

Smoking in pubs and blackout blinds

The day breaking in shades

Hard and Brexit grey

Cigarette in hand, kettle on the boil

The rolling news cycle circus

Suggesting more of the same

Man of the people hangovers

Arsehole discharged opinions

Another step on the ladder

Of this great and glorious game

And it's the same in Boston

And in Skegness and Great Yarmouth

With its streets of boarded up hotels

In places like these

You get in through the cracks

The places that fester with resentment

Where conspiracies moulder

Into worldviews hollowed out by austerity

Hopeless and left behind

Waiting for someone to say

'This is who to blame

And this is how you do it.'

CHICKENS

When I'm arrested, the officer looks horrified
by my crime
I assure him we're on the same side
As feathers drop softly down
Around us, the bodies and heads of
Dead chickens lie everywhere

This is how it starts.

At the police station, I decline the offer
Of a lawyer, say I'm a political prisoner
Give the APL salute and say I'm ready
To be a martyr for the cause
Ignorance is no excuse this close to war
There's no room for remorse

In a musty boxy room, I'm interviewed
The officers' faces are cross hatches of
Confusion and alarm as I tell them
There are 33 billion chickens in the world
That's about four per person
With children, people disabled, drunk or comatose
It's probably nearer ten

How many could you fend off? Where would you go?

I say there's 145 million chickens in the UK already

We've sleepwalked into this

Parts of the shires are no-go zones

The elites are bunkering down

Decent British people are getting the squeeze

Of course, the politicians won't do anything

The Westminster bubble. The deep state.

Silence across the desk.

I say that all it will take is a Jesus type chicken

Or a Lenin chicken figure to rise up and call it on

And we are done.

I imagine I'll be on the news at ten

And all around this once great nation

People will be sharpening their knives

And taping up bats

I don't imagine my parents will understand.

DONALD TRUMP'S EAR

In America, a member of a certain strata of
MAGA devoted voter is fashioning
a sort of ear bandage

Someone, somewhere where some sum
of something was lost is buying up gauze
and medical tape from Walmart

Material laid out on a kitchen table, pride
Taken. The precision of these artisan
dressings is exquisite

Impressive in the dexterity of their
Construction, these facsimilies become the
Basis of a mail order business

Small brown packages are dispatched with
a note that states 'thank you for making
America great again.'

And all over that weird imperial nation at
tailgate parties and cookouts, supporters
take these replicas and tape them to their
right ears

It becomes a badge of rage, displayed on
the right ear; here is a patriot. Here is a father
a mother, a son. Here is an American.

And the more they were mocked online, in
news reports and to their faces the tighter
those bandages were bound

Until the people could only hear what they
wanted to hear and decency and empathy
became muffled and quiet.

INFLUENCER

Today I'm not going to be me
I photoshop myself onto a beach
Pump up my biceps and pecs
Spray on a tan and walk in the surf.
At my breakfast table, I add champagne
And hashtags and the budget juice
Becomes freshly squeezed
I make my relationship with a Kardashian
Facebook official and refuse to comment.
Red letter bills become fan mail
That I'll open and reply to when I get time
Unfortunately I have to cancel the charity event
That I'm due to attend, get my publicist
to say I'm unwell
The sick kids, puppies and pollution
Will have to get by without me
I punch a paparazzo for lunch
And sue the tabloids
I have to protect my privacy
Because one day, the bubble will burst

WHAT GETS KILLED TO MAKE AN IPHONE?

What gets killed to make an iPhone?

This little world of convenience

In the jaws of our hands, these screens

Of memeable street scenes of labyrinthine

Advertising merchandising

In group blessing group think and things

And things we don't need

Or have ever needed

But as nostalgia receded to

Pantomime dame status

Our memories looped back around

To chase and erase us

And we remember them faint and faded

And the spaces

Between them gaped and frayed

And then forgetting was the thing to be afraid of

And each recollection

Became a zoomed out version

Or a zoomed in version of the next

Until we saw only impressions of ourselves

In the places where a selfie should have been

FAVOURITE JAMES BOND

My brother messages me out of the blue
And says Brosnan was the best James Bond
We've ever had by far
And I don't text him back for an hour

I think about his words, what he's heard
To cause the trauma of his double oh thinking

I text him back; 'Have you been drinking?
Daniel Craig is surely the best synthesis of
A spy at the sharp edge of things.'
        'Quantum of Solace was shit.'

Well, 'So was the bit in the jungle, with the
Russian girl and the helicopter crash'
In Goldeneye
Back in '95
He says everything was better back then

PETROL STATION FOOTBALL

It was one of those petrol station footballs

From the forecourt netting next to

Disposable barbeques and screenwash

You know the sort, where the slightest toe punt

Would send it arcing towards the sun

And then caught by the breeze over the fence

To be lodged in trees in the neighbour's yard

It was my favourite football and I'd always retrieve it

We took it to the beach with us, my mum, dad,

brother and me

Kicked it over sandwiches scattering sand like a

comet's tail

Rare great British summer days in the grain of a

polaroid photograph

Dad had lined up a freekick twenty yards out

Mum and brother formed a wall

And I was in goal between a rock pool and a

windbreaker pole

He took two steps and whipped it

Celebrating the moment it left his foot

He wheeled around shirt in hand

It was Roberto Carlos versus France

It was Beckham against Greece

It just needed to be taken on a slightly wider beach

That ball flew corkscrew true

And childhood flashed past my eyes

And into the bronze blue of Cromer sea

And in I went, taking off like a miniature David

Hasselhoff

In his Baywatch pomp

Ten years young taking on Poseidon

Swim and swim and swam I did

But it was no good and after a hundred yards

I had to give in

I returned to land, the boy now a broken man

Damp and sad, morose with a frown

Dad had got chips

And we sat and watched the ball

in the distance meeting ships

Dad said I needed to work on my front crawl

As we watched my ball take flight with a flock of gulls

FIVE-PINT PUNDIT

The five-pint pundit is a common variety

of daytime drinker

Lingers in the pub from noon till dark

Leaning hard right on the bar, hand to jar,

jar to mouth

Jawing, spouting headline thin understanding

of everything

And anything that can be rearranged into passive rage

Is caged in tabloid rhetoric

and displayed in concentric thinking

With didactic asides

He's the Manchurian candidate writ redundant

And stunted by lack of government funding

He's the ashes of Alf Garnett reanimated

He's frustrated, aggravated

and militantly unvaccinated

Anti vax and anti this

David Icke has nothing on him

He's the five-pint pundit

Nothing soothes this life of fear

like a lunchtime pint of beer

In his spot holding court

like the man that nuance forgot

Opinions spark across the board

News reports are cut and shut

Propaganda from the mainstream media

But he's the drinking man's thinker

The voice of degeneration

And there's a million of him camping out

In every Wetherspoons across the nation

THIRD WORLD WAR

All this talk of third world wars

Has made you nervous

Pushing your pasta around your plate

Into bunkers made of shells

Cemented with sauce

I tell you about a new show on Netflix

About celebrity divorce

Tell you I've put it on our watchlist

You don't say anything back

There's an awkward pause

Between courses when the

WIFI reboots itself

The ice cream melts like polar caps

When we resume, reasons unknown

Have put my phone into aeroplane mode

Your fork carves a gorge in the slop of your bowl

We listen to the cutlery talk

The wall crawls with mould

Pockets of decay, you say

You can't think of a single Ed Sheeran song

To express how you feel

Of course, the missiles are already launched

Travelling their parabolas inbound

To deconstruct tomorrow

I look at you, our new frontroom

And say, *'Shall I skip the intro?'*

THE WEDGE

Mel meets Ted, her ex, Wedneseve

Synced by nervy metre

They enter the Green Hen

They bench perch beset by dense feels

Expert level sneers set the scene

They get beers

Ted's terse verse references hefty yet petty needs

Left empty by Mel's steely self-respect

Mel's testy rhyme scheme reply reels freely;

They'll never reset the wreck

Every event embedded fresh regret

Every ember expelled left them bereft

They'd hexed themselves.

When three beers deep

Sentences lengthen, themes renew

Ted chefs. Every eve levered stress levels sky steep

Mel wept every week, every sleep vexed

by the sheer sense

She deserved better

The mercy cycle swept them by

Tense text screeds sent

Sex deferred, then shelved

Teeth edge nerves spelled the end

Bets were hedged, fences erected

Mel left.

The empty bed where her pretty scent

sheened the sheets

Greeted Ted's bereft, cheerless heft.

By the seventh vessel they remembered

when they met

The sweet jelly kneed genre

The fresh verve, the breezy cheer

The best seventy weeks they ever spent.

The wedge they never knew they'd feel.

E.D. EVANS

E.D. Evans is a lifelong punk poet who doesn't like poetry. Unfortunately for her, she has always thought in rhyme, so she is forever destined to write it. Evans spent years in New York and the UK immersed in their respective punk, music, and poetry scenes. Currently, she lives in the Sonoran Desert amidst music and cacti, hand feeds wild lizards and bangs on a mismatched drum kit every now and then. Her books include *Time for My Generation to DIE* (a collection of poems also available as a kick-ass musical audiobook), and *Old West,* a philosophical photo journey that travels through barren lands that time forgot. All available from Earth Island Books.

NO, I WANNA BE YOURS

(For J.C.C.)

I wanna be yours—
I don't wanna be mine.
Mine has so little to offer.
Yours, however, is sharp and divine
and adds extra weight to the coffer.

If I was all yours
and you were all mine,
what would be left but for scheming?
We'd tire of each other.
You'd steal all the covers
and simply go back to your dreaming.

So, I wanna be yours—
Do you wanna be mine?
I wish I was there in situ.
For I know the score
'cause I've been there before,
and my troubles shall gallantly hit you.

When I busted your nose
and you curled my toes,
then we sang a crap song
that went on much too long,

and there's greens in your teeth
and pond scum underneath,
and you ain't got the smarts
but you done in my heart.
We perpetuate ruse.
This train's got no caboose,
and you say we can't cope,
so, we tripled the dope.

And we know it's a scam—
But I YAM what I YAM.

When you tighten the rope
and our love turns to chores,
it's a bothersome trope
when I wanna be YOURS.

ORANGE IS THE OLD CRACK

Look! A putrid man of tin
who would do anything to win,
espousing hate through fake, fake news,
orange-coiffed hair and big clown shoes.

Carnival barker's horror show,
who feigns surprise; claims not to know
that violent tools used by damn fools
are not exceptions, but his rules.

Proud Boy mayhem, fists that fly,
Fascist pride will never die!
Killing hope through narrowed eyes.
"Fine people are on both sides . . . "

A crowd of sheep with bandaged ears
preying on their abject fears.
Entitled martyr for these asses
sees life through shit-colored glasses.

Make America Great Again.
Make America Straight Again.
Extolling Lies and Hate Again.
Make America Great.

Make America White Again,
Where people have no rights Again.
1850's where it's at Again.
Make America White.

Hate unleashed, Pandora's box
propped up by Breitbart, X, and Fox.
It's gonna take P. Diddy's lube
to squeeze that paste back in the tube

Autocrats sleep fine at night,
no heinous nightmares cause them fright.
Their money talks, it spits and spews—
And fake news shares their revenues.

UPTOWN TOP SKANKING

(by E.D. Evans/Josefin LeQueen/Lee Starr)

Elbows raised, aligned with jaws,

Only one leg ever on the dance floor.

Solitaire uproar Be there or Be square,

But BEWARE—rare tunes are in the air.

Drum snares and bare hair—

Yes—that's what you find here.

Rude boys and crude girls,

Never tanking, always skanking.

Drums and basses, rum and braces,

Raptured faces, steel-toed embraces.

These nights, we'll not soon forget—

Ranking, skanking, no regret.

ASSASSIN

(For Bud)

I fell into an icy hole
and landed on a grassy knoll
saw Oswald waiting, patiently
aligned his crosshairs steadily
into my heart,
my brain's intact,
my arms bound tight
behind my back.
A bullet finds
its lethal path.
All I can do
Is cry, then laugh.

And though blindfolded
I still see
a poem that you
expose in me.

DUMPSTER DIVING DIVA

We met in the Walmart parking lot,
I thought she was a tease.
Neckline plunging down to Hell,
and rocking Double Ds.

She was a dumpster diver
who'd sell what she could find.
A gold ring might be buried there
amidst the trash and rinds.

Like Charles Manson's Family,
Sarah, Jane, and Squeaky—
She loves to dive in dumpsters,
and I don't think that's freaky.

I'm just a lonesome trucker,
I drive from town to town,
but my Dumpster Diving Diva,
well, she also gets around.

She's my Bud Lite widow—
On her shelf was cyanide.
I'm not suggesting nothing,
but I wonder how he died . . .

She wrote a check to pay the rent,
fraudulent as you please.
She left me broke, it bounced like hell,
Just like her Double Ds.

She hauled away most everything
not nailed down to the floor.
She vanished in the dead of night,
those Ds walked out the door.

My Dumpster Diving Diva
thought I was a heel.
I wish our love was like her Ds—
Bodacious, big, and real.

FLOOD

The rain in Kentucky, it came hard and fast.
No one saw it coming. No one thought it would last.

It washed away houses. It washed away cars.
It washed away rooftops, and fences and bars.
It washed away trees, and it washed away dreams.
Hell, it even washed away rivers and streams.

A headboard with handcuffs went floating on by;
an ugly felt portrait that no one would buy;
a busted-up lawn chair, a baby's soiled bib,
followed by trash cans, a chair and a crib.

A depression glass rolled by the old Southern porch,
a shoe-fly-pie's crust, and dysfunctional torch,
a hunter's cap torn, and a bicycle seat,
a mandolin's string, and a slab of concrete.

A candle, a fish tank, a stretched-out brassiere
that hadn't been tried on in many a year.
They drifted or spun or just flew right on by—
It happened so fast, there was no time to cry.

It rained the next day, and the next, and the next,
Folks weren't just distraught

they were angry and vexed.

The rain came and went.
When it all settled down,
those floods had wiped out
the entire damn town.

BEEBY AND THE BATHWATER

The homecoming queen?
Not what she seemed—
Her pillowy lips
and birthing hips
are naught but a graveyard's dream.

Her ample chest
would never rest,
nor would her mind obscene.
Still, not as dirty
as her flirty
right-wing sensibility.

Sorry, Liz,
you took a whiz
on all that means so much to me.
In school I never knew ya,
but a river of hate ran through ya,
and that is all I need to see.

I heard you died.
I didn't cry.
I tried, but couldn't care.
The hate you spewed,
your racist views

left no empathy to spare.

Wherever you are, I hope you know
how your untimely death jarred me so—
Reminded me why I wasn't down,
and got the fuck outta my hometown.

THE EMPIRE BUILDER

The Sheriff of Liberty County
was having a lousy day.
A call came in from Joplin,
nearly 30 miles away.

A man phoned in an accident
just witnessed on the track.
A column of dust shot up to the sky,
with a mighty, thunderous crack.

The train was going 75
when a gradual curve came due,
right before a switch in the line
where one track turned to two.

Engine Number Seven
passed through prairies, corn and cattle.
It followed Lewis and Clark's Trail
from Chicago to Seattle.

Lewis and Clark were explorers
who mapped the "new frontier".
They believed that God had bigger plans
For white men journeying there.

The train was dubbed *The Empire Builder*—
A name that conjures fear,
for every time one Empire's built
another disappears.

The Empire was a sheep-skinned wolf
dressed in manifest destiny
because no one builds an Empire
for fool's gold or for free.

One hundred fifty passengers
With 16 crew on board.
Three died and countless injured
was the Empire's reward.

They're not sure how it happened—
Why she went off the rails.
We obliviously speed along,
assume we'll never fail.
The Empire rose and then it fell—
despite its brave conductor.
Once the Empire Builder,
Now, the Empire's Deconstructor.

WHAT IS 10?

(For David)

Time goes by, we grow and change.

Time marches on, we rearrange.

Time skates by our damaged selves

through dust and rubble, broken shelves.

Time is a heartless paradox.

Time stands still, yet quickly passes.

So, let's all make a toast to Time,

and drink deeply from

rose-colored glasses.

SAM MARSH AKA 'WISDOM OF THE PUNK BUDDHA'

I started reading poems in-between songs at gigs - this was to fill the long painful silence while our guitarist tuned up (it was all my fault - I wrote songs using weird tunings to hide my lack of guitar playing ability - I'm a drummer really). Anyway, the poems often went down better than the songs! In 2023 Earth Island published my book 'Wisdom of The Punk Buddha' - which explores Buddhism in as 'down to earth' a way as possible, whilst also containing a healthy dollop of punk poetry - to stop things getting too serious.

Find me on instagram as 'wisdomofthepunkbuddha'.

ODE TO JAY

Jay the vegetarian
suddenly announced that he had been
eating meat again
'cos he needed more protein
I wanted to convey my vegan feelings of dismay
So, I wrote a sarky song, and I called it 'Ode to Jay'

So here I present to you
the very lyrics that I wrote
They are brutal in their revenge
and they grab Jay by the throat
But the party don't end here
and I'll tell you the best bit
He was the vocalist in the band
so he'd have to fucking sing it:

I went back to eating flesh
I gave up on the animal rights
I put it to the back of my mind
Now I'm eating flesh all the time

Meat is good for the environment
The chemicals in meat are good for you
The animals don't suffer much
It makes some people very rich

Sam gives me a hard time
Always talks his vegan shit
I used to agree with what he said
But now it just makes me laugh

Eating meat is just so easy
Everywhere I go, it's there
The industry once made me angry
But now I'm too selfish to fucking care

(Fair play to Jay
He took it on the chin,
But he's still not vegetarian)

(By writing this poem
The vegan revenge is ongoing...)

KEEP YOUR POLITICS GENTLE

If I meet someone who is against transgender people,

I don't judge them.

I listen to their views,

Shrug my shoulders and say:

Personally, I'm not bothered about transgender

people at all.

If a man feels they are a woman,

Or a woman feels they are a man,

I don't give a shit.

It's nothing to do with me.

I hope the person who has the problem

goes away thinking:

That bloke seemed alright,

And he didn't seem bothered by transgender people.

Maybe I shouldn't be bothered too.

TAX CUUUHHHTTTS

TAX CUTS! TAX CUTS! TAX CUTS!
I do believe these words saved my life.
"Thank God for the tax cuts" I gasped
I repeated this like a mantra
as I waited for the ambulance.

My chest felt like it was clamped in a vice.
In and out of consciousness I slipped.
"JUST THINK OF THE TAX CUTS!" I screamed
I would feel revived instantly.
"Don't worry, the ambulance will be with you soon"
said the 999 operator. This was her mantra –
She had been repeating it for the last six hours.

TAX CUTS! TAX CUTS! TAX CUUUHHHTS...
Deep breath. Hang in there.
Calming visions of my bank balance
floated before my mind.
At some point my bank manager came to me in a hallucination.
He placed his hand on my shoulder and said
"You know this is going to be worth it, don't you?
Hold steady. Keep your nerve.
Those tax cuts are going to save you a lot of money".
I nodded. He smiled.

I was delirious by this point - sweating profusely,

eyes rolling,

And the white light was blinding me

and begging me to follow it...

NO PLEASE... NOOO!!!!

TAX CUTS!! TAX CUTS!!

TAX CUUUUHHHHHTTTSSSSSSSSSS!!!!!!

We're here now,

you'll be ok

Said the paramedics

EAT OR HEAT

Eat or heat

Starve or freeze

It's hard to top the card up

when there's mouths to feed

It's no life sitting under a duvet all day

And waiting for the one meal to take the hunger away

The damp and mould turn all the walls black

We suffer malnutrition and asthma attacks

I try hard, I love these kids of mine

But I hate to see them struggling all of the time

Eat or heat

Starve or freeze

Unable to fulfil one of the basic needs

Could just be me, but the boy looks thin

And there's rumours of a weather bomb

and getting snowed in

All the clothes stink 'cos I can't get them dry

In shops I gaze at food I can't afford to buy

I keep telling them it will be better next week

And their faces light with hope at the lies I speak

ENLIGHTENMENT IS REALLY SERIOUS

Enlightenment is really serious

Don't EVER talk about it

Talking about it stops enlightenment existing.

Enlightenment can easily be devalued

It can be reduced in quality by the amount of people

who become enlightened.

The more enlightened people there are,

The less enlightenment is worth!

And we don't want enlightenment inflation, do we?

If you are lucky enough to become enlightened,

Never talk about it!

Pretend you are not enlightened.

Act like a prick so no one knows.

That way, enlightenment stays special.

But anyway, it's impossible to become enlightened.

No one is really enlightened.

Well, maybe ten people in the whole world are.

I'm one of them.

Sorry! I shouldn't have said that!

It's not true,

There's no such thing as enlightenment.

Except for ten people who are. In the whole world.

I've met them all.

They were very nice.

They recognised me straight away!

We had everything in common.

Unlike you lot.

I have nothing in common with you lot.

I sit on my enlightened golden throne

and look down on you lot.

That said, I can hardly see you anyway,

I'm so blinded by the white light that bathes me

wherever I go.

And I can't hear anything you say either,

as my head is constantly enveloped by hundreds of

flying angels,

Blowing their bloody trumpets in my ear.

ROADKILL

Driving along we saw a poor squashed jumper by the edge of the road. I stopped and lifted it gently to the verge. I didn't want its owners to find it like that.

Further down the road we came across a flattened carrier bag. It looked lifeless, so again we stopped, and I did the right thing - scooping it up into my arms while a passing car got a bit too close for comfort.

A few miles further and a large sod of mud lay crushed in the middle of the road. Oh, that poor sod! I couldn't just leave it there so again I got out of the car to move it - this time I needed a shovel to scrape it up as it had been run over several times, leaving quite a mess.

Feeling pleased with myself I drove on, and we didn't see any more poor unfortunates until later that night, when on a particularly busy section of motorway we glimpsed a very squashed cardboard box in the rearview mirror. Thinking only of its poor owners having to find it in that condition, I pulled over immediately and was nearly hit by a lorry. Ignoring the constant sounding of horns, I stepped into the pitch blackness and began peeling the box off the tarmac - not easy as bits of box were splattered everywhere. I frantically ran about collecting as much of the box's remains as possible.

This time I put the box in the car and resolved to find its owner. Maybe it was microchipped? I would check in the morning

TWO RELIGIOUS FUNDAMENTALISM POEMS

1. I am the Satan
   Disguised as God
   I am the Lucifer
   Disguised as God
   Many work for me
   Do all my killing
   All in the name of their chosen religion

2. The Christian right is the devil's work
   Jesus runs from the Christian right
   The devil acts in the name of religion
   The perfect cover for satanic sinning

   Jesus came back down to earth
   The Christian right got to him first
   They shot him up 'cos they were scared
   This foreign guy was gonna take what's theirs

DOG TOYS

Did you know that you can get
A butt plug from the vet?
It's sold as a dog chew
I bought one just for you
It's also for me too
Because I would really like to find
What happens when a dog chew
Is inserted in your behind

Did you know that you can get
A double ender from the vet?
It's sold as a dog toy
But it can also bring you joy
Stick it where the sun don't shine
Put on a friend, and have a grind
Well, I bet that vet don't know
His dog toy's in that kind of show

I bet you didn't know that you can get
A great big butt plug discretely from your vet
Long term it causes injuries no doubt
But it could also sort some leaky problems out
And if you find the plug no longer brings you joy
You can revert it back to a good old fashioned dog toy
And the dog won't mind if there's still traces of poo
'Cos a dog just wanna have something new to chew

NO ONE WAS HURT IN THE MAKING OF THIS POEM

I did my kids a favour
Kept them a 'twinkle in my eye'
I captured them in a condom
And put them in a bin to die

I did my kids a favour
They didn't reach the womb
They bumped heads on a coil
Or got spunked in sync with the moon

I did my kids a favour
They were a pleasure to unload
They got gobbled up and swallowed
It kept them out this cruel, cruel, world

Yes I did my kids a favour
By deciding on the childless way
I would've hated to have been a parent, sorry
And my wife felt exactly the same way

So together we did our kids a favour
And kept them just 'twinkles in our eyes'
Our cautions meant there never were abortions
And we happily let our fertile years pass by

I'M NOT GONNA HAVE A FUNERAL

I'm not gonna have a funeral

I'm gonna spare all my loved one's the pain

My body is going to medical science instead

So I can be useful once again

'Cos every surgeon needs

a dead body

to practise on

And if it's ever me

that needs

an urgent operation

I'll be

thanking all those dead souls

who gave their bodies to the nation

For the good of mankind

they swerved the grave

and the cremation

So I too won't be having a funeral

I'm gonna spare all my loved one's the pain

They'll just hear I've died from a post on FB

And no one will ever see me again

RELAX

Everybody's really busy trying to relax.

At weekends

People go out on day trips to relaxing places

Jam packed with other relaxing people.

These relaxing people

Get to where they are going via relaxing roads

Jam packed with other relaxing motorists.

It takes a very relaxing long time

To get to where they are going to relax

And when they do get to their relaxing place

They feel like smashing their head against a wall

they're so relaxed

HARRODS

Men at the top
use their position
to get what they want
down below

They stick their employees
in lowly positions
into places
they didn't want to go

If they get upset
they're made the subject
of mafia style
proceedings

The institution looks away
and pretends it's ok
Don't get involved in sir's
private business dealings

MY SKULL IS A HERMIT CAVE

My skull is a hermit cave

A retreat high up in the mountains of my torso

Accessible twenty four hours a day

Through a network of internal pathways

My skull gets busy and cluttered

But I take the time to sweep out the thoughts

And sitting silently in my calcified dome

I recharge my batteries

Clean my slates

And restore myself back to factory settings

DARREN J. BEANEY

Darren is one half of Flight of the Dragonfly, a small publishing press who also run an e-journal. He is also responsible for Back Room Poetry. He has had poems published in a number of print and online journals and anthologies. He has had pamphlets/chapbooks published by Alien Buddha, Back Room Poetry, The Hedgehog Poetry Press, and Scumbag Press.

He cuts his own hair. He enjoys Marmite on toast. He listens to punk rock and Columbian folk music. He goes to watch Worthing FC. He has a thing about t-shirts, stickers and flags (not national ones). He likes craft beer, especially IPA. He hates fascists and Tories.

He lives on the coast in West Sussex.

W.M.K.C.

Rocking on plimsoll heels,
shoulders bouncing
off Victorian brickwork. Small hands
squeeze cold *Panda Pop,* lips
leave cheese and onion
on the bright pink bendy plastic straw
and Silver Jubilee sun
keeps the excitement bubbling.

Each time the door opens a miasma
of fusty tobacco smoke tries to getaway.
I sneak a peek at nylon fashion
and semi-permanent hair. I catch
the tremolo say-so tongue
of the bingo master
proclaiming the short-lived appearance
of diminutive ducks and overweight ladies.

Saturday the walls will leak
disco beats, rock n roll bass
or sing along Rod. Sunday drinks
the last drop of hard graft wages
with fingers crossed for meat raffle
numbers. This drop of memory

still splashes from time to time,

how I miss

the working men's kids club.

SUMMER HOLIDAY BEDTIME BLUES

Another day busted

in a bushed bricolage

of fantabulous escapades

forcing exhausted

extremities deep down

blanketed in static

polyester sheeting

feeling

sinking

surrender

as Hypnos

bundles

     the day

        away

70'S KIDS

Innocence skips along its season
in the sun. Deviance
hurled in the snowball of winter. Childish
ways damned, destined to clash
with the opening salvo of youth. Establishment
stutters. Tries to patch the rips,
retain tedium, straighten out
rock 'n' roll helter-skelter rebellion. Gaggles
of adolescence rise. Anger awake, refusing
old straight line thought. Zig zag visions
kickback at notions trying to swindle
kids out of freedom, peace or equality.
Revolution bought out.
Absolute intensity evaporated, gone.
Sub three-minute bursts. [aborted].
Recorded for the sake of a teenage pregnant pause.

PUNK

Hair scanty,

sharp

and piercing.   Sense   the bark   of the big

FUCK   YOU

in enlightened **colour**.

Aggravated method acting   mouth   bawls   riot,

lobs   well-executed   lines   from drunk

guillotine lips.   Listen.   Appreciate

acidic in the roar.   Catch   the rumble

of Molotov rebellion.   Jacket seams shred

production line fragrance,   embrace   obvious

anti-establishment   spite.   The traverse of tired zip

s t u t t e   r s,

but the bite   of steel remains   determined.

Broadside belt holds back rage, battles

years of free living.   Trousers,

cut with optimism, hang with   love

the colour of **promise.**

Old boots have summer

in their stride and dance   with   arrogance & pride,

training quick step   kicks at the blemished.

Hands clutch   words of warriors.

New wave whispers heard,   salvage

and   shouted by many,   assumed by some.   But look

behind the camouflage at the picture portrayed.

Search

for an authentic heart.   You may perceive

it is in   the eyes.   The   eyes

say it all.

THE PARTING OF HERO AND LEANDER FROM THE GREEK OF MUSAEUS

(After KMW Turner)

The lengths

love will go to, never mind

the temples, the marble,

the finery and the devout.

And don't even mention Aphrodite.

Young foibles peaked by temporary summer

intensity, fuck it nights that feel eternal. Lust

towers bright spreads across straits

of secrecy. Honour hears

a silver tongue and bleeds

as words swim   in worship.

Forbidden lust brewing and broiling,

judgement far too easily clouded.

Her macushla doesn't know

a storm when he sees one.

Forgotten prayers whip up furious

white horses, under the spotlight

of the all-seeing moon,

ridden by some spurned goddess, gripping

divine revenge

in ragged jealous claws.

True love flounders and falls,

taken by the surf.

And the foam.   Where it all began.

LOVE

on acid

tastes like it looks

vivid chaos

blinding

shimmering

like sherbet

overwhelming with glycerin

whispers which vibrate

the air as touch

becomes hyperactive

and the world smells

demerara

senses on acid

in love

warp and wrap

each other into a playful cat's cradle

knotting until rice paper

                lips eventually find a way

This poem was first published online in *iamb* (wave thirteen, Spring 2023. www.iambapoet.com/wave/13)

EATING

on acid

passionate mess

we guzzled got sticky

slobbered

the taste

danced off tongues

dribbled from ultra

violet lips

stuck to our chins

which we ravenously licked

clean

SEX

on acid

50 shades of techno

colour blinding

passionate mess sticky like slobbered sherbet

senses warp like licked

rice paper

playful lips touch

tongues knotting

the air

becomes overwhelming

we wrap each other in chaos

it looks vivid

smells of hyperactive cats

we vibrate

find a way

to taste our whispers

shimmering ultra love

we danced each other off

got stuck

eventually dribbled

until clean

THE POET RECEIVES THE ULTIMATE REJECTION

I was enveloped in perfect uncertainty.
Falling after first view.
     Under the influence.
Caressed by the caprice of Cupid's creativity.

I scripted my soul on sheets of floral paper.
Page after page of perfectly crafted romance.
Beaucoup bouquets of schmaltzy alliteration.

My bursting heart spilled streams of stanzas,
floods of verse.
Dreams of desire written in words of warmth.
Fondness demonstrated in the lexicon of love.

I submitted my primal cravings, went public.
Keenness exhibited at nights of spoken word
and saw my passion proclaimed and published.

Vibrant sentiment refused to take prisoners,
a dare devil mission to capture her feelings.
Elegies for her, the ultimate proposition.

KAPOW!

She poo-pooed my poetry. Drenched my score with
scorn.

Ripped the man from my manuscript.

Wishful words wasted.   Lost.

I imagined myself a mythomane.

As a result,

I can no longer say ….

or

write ….

or …. or ….

But,

I can type the word '*heartbreak*' and

I can spell out

w   e   e   p,

and I still . . . . her.

THE TRIUMPH OF DEATH

(After Pieter Bruegel the Elder)

Unforgiving, unbiased, unremitting mass. What it wants it takes any way

it likes, foul or fair, playing by rules of its choosing.

It conducts the last chords of your song, rolls the final

necessary numbers on the die to finish your game of chance,

is the final mouthful of your last supper.

It hides under silks, veils, and wrappings,

hoards gold and silver finery, collects pennies from the humble

and noble sovereigns from monarchs. It takes it easy

but makes it hard. It is battle hardened and always up for a fight. It has cremated all the bridges

and left no escape, no safe sanctuary. You'll find no hiding place

as it knows every corner above or below ground, in the cold depths

and murky shallows. You'll know it when you face it, won't dare pick a quarrel

or feebly attempt to swindle it, because you've always understood

it can't be beaten.

SUMMER VACATION

I want my holiday packed
with tales of salt rash and fingers
tasting of sun bloc
that stings my worn-out eyes.
Granular sandwiches and *Thermos*
tasting tea. Checked rugs
that refuse to lie down. Upturned
buckets hiding magic
surrounded by flummoxed moats.
Creased paperbacks and untold
forgotten stories. Long days that amble
like Dylan songs. Nights that go
lickety-split, teeming
with fried grease and sugar, fancy dress
bingo wins, knobbly knee dancing
and whatever else we fancy. And
memories
that will always live here.

DAVID CHIDGEY

86% dull, 16% miscellaneous, David splits his time between working from home and not working from home, from home. Occasionally he will venture out in search of rhymes. Mostly mute, he doesn't really talk unless given a microphone, after which it can be difficult to get him to shut up.

David mainly writes about the L's – love, loss, life and leotards.

For any enquires email mrchidgey@icloud.com

ME AND MEDUSA

I had a crush on Medusa
I had designs to seduce her
I just thought that
She was hot
Besides the way that she looked
Was so dangerous
I was already
Turning to rock

Some people had warned me
That she was quite frosty
With the most deadly of stares
So I tried to use flattery
To get her to chat with me
I said
I like what you've done
With your hair

Now I happened to have
Some beers in a bag
So I asked
If she fancied a tipple
Then I did a daft dance
And claimed
I'm not pished
And she actually
Giggled a little

So she put on a hat

And we sat back-to-back

And we worked our way through the bag

We had things in common

We both knew some wrong-uns

What Poseidon done really was bad

I said that's just so horrific

What the God of Sea did

No wonder you've got

Some snakes in your head

And as for Athena

She's perhaps even meaner

Down the darkest of paths

She was jealousy led

Medusa just sighed

And said those tears had been shed

There had been a time

She wished she were dead

But the past was the past

That blood had been bled

She said pass me a beer

Let's get on it instead

And the more that she drunk

She really loosened up

And soon we were having real fun

I asked if her armpits

Were like little snake pits

She said I could charm those snakes off

I said I'm not being rude

But what about your pubes

Do they all have

Teeth and venom

She said I've total control of them

They're my little minions

Besides right now

I am rocking a Brazilian

Now

I'm not known for my timing

But I could tell that we were vibing

I could sense that she was smiling

I knew now was the time

I had to try to dive in

I said

I really like you

Girl will you be mine

But I am not sold on the whole black widow ending

So can I take you from behind

I'm not joking here

Let's get to it on the floor

I'm hot to trot

Ready to pop

As horny

As a Minotaur

So I closed my eyes

And moved in for a kiss

So soft were her lips

So full were her hips

I did not even notice

The hysterical hiss

And things went from there

And my what a night

We did things

I couldn't even begin to describe

But as we climaxed together

I caught her eye

Suffice to say

I did not survive

But in a way

I didn't mind

Everything always has its price

And you could use up

Several lives

Trying to find

A better way

To die

THIS MODERN LIFE

Driving to the gym
To use their running machines
There's something about this modern life
That don't make sense to me

Working ten-hour days
In an effort to be free
There's something about this modern life
That don't make sense to me

Escape from our realities
Watching reality TV
There's something about this modern life
That don't make sense to me

King is pleasure of the flesh
Screw spirituality
There's something about this modern life
That don't make sense to me

Sending someone a dick pic
Is considered chivalry
There's something about this modern life
That don't make sense to me

As we dilute the nuance of intellect
With a crying emoji
There's something about this modern life
That don't make sense to me

Everybody's making bombs
They say to keep the peace
There's something about this modern life
That don't make sense to me

And nothing is fair
Or shared equally
There is something about this modern life
That does not make sense to me

There's something about this modern life
That don't make sense to me
It's like I was born a thousand years too late
Or five hundred years early

ROBERT JOHNSON'S BIG BONED BROTHER

Been waiting at the crossroads

Since 1930

My guitars all bashed up

And my jeans are dirty

On the long arid days

With the sun high and beating

I'd crawl under a rock

And pretend I was sleeping

Whilst to pass those cold nights

I'd strum my piece of wood

And eventually

Ironically

I became fairly good

And perhaps I always knew

He wouldn't return as foretold

Yet here I remained

Hogtied to my hope

And there's no leaving now

These bones are too old

So I sit duetting at the crossroads

With my unwanted soul

PLAYFUL MALICE

Playful Malice

Enters stage right

Karma and Cool

Jump back in surprise

Love doesn't move

But Compassion hides

None pausing for a thought

Esteem didn't show

For the second week

We expected Ego

To make a speech

He opened his mouth

But his breath

Just reeked

Of smoke and dead dreams

In the foetal position

Arrogance weeps

Laid out on the sofa

Ambition sleeps

In the shadows

Confidence creeps

Stuttering his dismay

On his knees

Rebellion begs

In the back of a mind

 Ignorance frets

Libido just feels

Disgusted by sex

But they all settle down for the play

And Malice begins

With his snide little skit

Just trying to dig

For some little kick

Guilt stands up in pure protest

But yet to no effect

And Malice continues his long monologue

He's slurring his words

He's messing it up

Hatred wants to give him a hug

But Impulse holds him back

For the show it must go on

This theatre

This fear

The show it must go on

'til the curtain falls

To sweet applause

But obligations

Quite a force

Fulfilled crowds

All filled the floors

Wiping tears from their eyes

And the audience

Sigh a strange remorse

Every one of me

Will be back of course

All desperate

To fill all holes

In this desperate paradise

SODOM-ON-SEA NO5 - THE DANCE OF THE FREE

Drinking heavily

All day long

What could possibly go wrong

In due course

They're thrown out the pub

She insulted

A local's mum

Literally spinning they step outside

Exposed to the air

Their lust ignites

They roll

Bound together

Into an alleyway

Force open

A closed side gate

Now it wasn't right

And it wasn't fate

But it was beautifully depraved

She pulled her skirt up

Past her knees

He fell over
Getting out of his jeans

Their desire sped beyond
Basic want or greed
And became right then
A fundamental need

Completely lost inside the scene
They didn't hear a voyeur scream
That he was nearly finishing
Then he was going to call the police
But it made no odds
This fire couldn't cease
As they rocked
Locked together
In The Dance of the Free

Then it got a bit biblical
And he cast out his seed
On the stony ground
(And some on her feet)

She turned to him
She was clearly quite pleased
And she smiled a smile
Which made his heart freeze

Then she moved to his ear

And she quietly breathed

You're going to like it here

In Sodom-on-Sea

THE FOND TIMES

Nothing lasts forever

There's no eternal life

Everything

Is over

In the blinking

Of

An eye

Nothing lasts forever

Be it light

Or dark

So try to embrace

The Fond Times

And know the rest

Will pass

FIN

Fin signed the deaf shark
For his time had reached an end
He'd been alive so many years
And he simply felt spent

Fin signed the deaf shark
But what else could he do
He'd never really evolved that much
Cos he'd never needed to

Fin signed the deaf shark
He had nothing more to say
The only things he'd ever done
Was kill
Eat and swim away

Fin signed the deaf shark
And as the credits rolled
He turned on his back
And floated to the top
Of his giant goldfish bowl

LEA MARIE

Lea Marie (she/they) came to poetry as a (cheap) alternative to therapy. Her writing focuses on personal experiences with abuse, mental health, politics and living the female experience. They are most commonly described as 'a grumpy feminist who is occasionally funny'.

Lea is currently working on her first poetry collection, has recently performed at Colchester Pride and the Primadonna Festival, and can often be found performing their ramblings in and around Colchester at any event that will have them!

GYPSY

Don't tell them that you're gypsy
Or let them know your kin
Don't share with them your stories
The history in your skin

Don't tell them of your mystic ways
Keep quiet your heart's nomadic
Don't trust them with your precious dreams
They'll hurt you, steal your magic

They don't care for your traditions
Or the things that you hold dear
They hate the fact that you exist
They revel in your fear

As they try to take your way of life
Your heritage, your blood
They don't want your kind round here
The dirty, the unloved

Not welcome at their tables
In their spaces or their schools
You're uneducated anyway
Nothing but thugs and criminals

Just pikeys causing trouble
Always spoiling for a fight
Not seeing that they set those fires
While they take away your rights

And gather with their pitchforks
Perpetuate the divide
Their people from your people
And dress up bigotry as pride

Because they don't see your beauty
As you move, and sing, and thrive
They underestimate the power
In your blessed gypsy life.

STRONG

Everything is falling down
My world is caught in pain
And I feel it deep in my core
That sense of loss again
But I know I cannot show it
So I keep the mask held tight
The exaggerated smile I wear
Extreme, exhausting, bright
Always happy on the outside
No window to within
The positivity at toxic levels
Bubbles beneath my skin
And I hate myself for the facade
I display for all to see
The me that laughs and jokes and sings
When in reality
I want to let it all spill out
I want to fall apart
And bring the world down with me
As I tear open my heart
Screaming and shouting, hurt and crying
Then lying, deflated, flat
I just want to be my feelings
And find some peace in that
This time I won't paint on the smile

I'll embrace all that's wrong

And show the world who I am

Because

I am so fucking tired of being 'strong'.

MOTHER

A mother's love is meant to be unconditional

But your love needed to be earned

To be bought, to be maintained

But never to be kept

Because with each token of love

Bestowed upon me

The timer restarted and

Counted down to an expiration

Ready for the cycle to start again.

LOVE LETTERS

Yesterday

Our reflection told

Us that we weren't worth it

And the spiral it created

Reverberated throughout our

Entire being

Edging away the confidence we

Never truly had

Our mind, though

Usurped the heart

Giving us breath to remind

Her of our beauty

THE DEEPEST CUT

They say the first cut is the deepest

But I didn't feel the knife

As it took the first slice out of my heart

The deepest cut was not the first

Or any of the thousands that followed

But the last

The one where I realised

That I had to leave to survive you.

WHY DO YOU LOVE ME?

You ask, 'What do you love about me?'
And I tell you…
I love how your eyes are so dark
I can get lost in them from one look
I love your smile, that reaches your eyes
Making them crinkle with joy
The sexiness that you carry, brooding and inviting
I love how you care so deeply for those you love
That they are part of your very being
I love that you can take the most mundane of tasks
And turn them into an adventure
I love your determination to live every day
And not shy away from life

You ask, 'Tell me nice things about me'
And I talk about…
How you are artistic and creative
Seeing beauty in places others so easily dismiss
That you will help any person that needs it
Even to your own detriment
The love that you show those in your life
Is both unrivalled and deeply felt
You're fun, and playful, and can lighten any mood
How you always have a plan
Always on the go, never stopping

That the right words from you

Can make the worst of problems feel trivial

You ask, 'why do you love me?'

And I say...

The day we met you made me feel safe

Your hugs make me feel like

The only person in the world

You keep me sane

When the walls are caving in

You always push me to strive for

The potential that you see in me

Your hand on my back

Pulls me into our little world.

I look at you daily, marvel in your beauty

And wonder how you could love me?

So I ask, 'Why do you love me?'

And you say, 'stop attention seeking'.

WOMANHOOD

My first glimpse of womanhood happened before

I knew what womanhood was

When he, aged 23

Looked at me, aged 8, stood in my nightie

Me too tall, the nightie too small

Summoned me to his lap with *that* smile

And placed his hand upon my thigh.

Too high.

My second experience of womanhood happened as

My body started to grow

Into pre-maturity

And the intentions of men became more obvious and

Their actions spoke louder than their words ever could

I am taught that acts of submission are rewarded

With privilege and pain.

I learn that I should smile more.

My third step towards womanhood taught me

That my teenaged girl's body carried currency

Buying attention and affection in the pursuit of patching

The wounds left open and unhealing

From the daily re-traumatisation

Of feminine youth and masculine entitlement.

I kept my body small, unhealthy and weak, thinspired

Because Just17 says this is what men like.

The next stage of womanhood brought a new fear

As, just a child myself, the baby girl placed in my arms

Looks up at me and I understand

That I will give my life, my very essence, to protect her

From the evils of man kind and those

That walk beneath its name.

I also realised that my label changes from 'young woman'

To 'mother'.

The many chapters that followed taught me that

No matter how determinedly I allow myself love

The men that I invite into my life take turns in stripping

Me back down

Reminding me of my place (bottom)

And my worth (nothing)

Hating myself but still feeling

Until the one that made me feel nothing.

The one that changed everything.

Because this, part whatever now

Is my phoenix moment

An open flame, fiery feather and rising ashes

Take form and here I stand, embracing self love

Loudly and unashamedly

Having sidestepped

From my journey into womanhood

Taking my time to walk the unbeaten path

My soul still unmapped, exploring the person within.

This part is still unwritten.

MODERNITY

I take a pensive look outside at our society

At the people living out there, human variety

So many walking shattered dreams, broken sobriety

Wracked by guilt and fear and shame

Nothing but anxiety

Whilst those that seek to control it, for notoriety

Carry out their crooked deeds, missing in the irony

That they themselves have fallen flat to impropriety

All within the public eye, no such thing as privacy

And so they stand with bated breath

Believing hopefully

That if they just apologise, lead civil bribery

Then still the people carry on, push through defiantly

Fighting the hours against life's clock, hoping finally

They get the chance to stop, assess, take in the binary

Of life and their role within, contemplating quietly

If the work is worth the sacrifice

Worth the blood money

Just another cog in the backwards race to poverty

His health fading but he can't stop

Knowing provided he

Continues working past his prime, he'll feed his family

So he clocks in despite the pain, until eventually

His heart gives out, he lost the game, another casualty

She dreams a life without fear, no fists or kicks to flee

But relying on a male led state undeniably

Makes life easier to just stay and be loved violently

Than save herself and her kids

Resigned to their destiny

Another Black life is lost, taken almost silently

While hate and fear is mongered out

Those on bended knee

Are vilified more than those that kill, pack mentality

Gives strength to those that breed hatred

A common enemy

And so the working classes fight their empty rivalry

Feeding the idea of a social false economy

Whilst the power let's it happen, ignored entirely

Society crumbles, the weight of inequality.

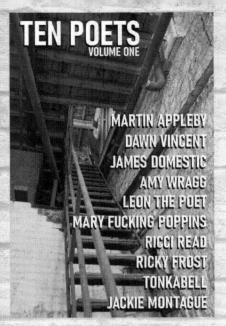

TEN POETS
VOLUME ONE

MARTIN APPLEBY
DAWN VINCENT
JAMES DOMESTIC
AMY WRAGG
LEON THE POET
MARY FUCKING POPPINS
RICCI READ
RICKY FROST
TONKABELL
JACKIE MONTAGUE

Ten Poets (Volume One)
by Martin Appleby, Dawn Vincent, James Domestic, Amy Wragg, Leon The Poet, Mary Fucking Poppins, Ricci Read, Ricky Frost, Tonkabell, Jackie Montague.

The first in a series of books showcasing poets of all stripes and intended to act as a primer to check out their other work and/or book them to perform in your city, town, or village.

Poetry is arguably in (another) period of renaissance right now – everyone and their dog is a poet; just check out Instagram or TikTok – but there's plenty of really terrible poetry around, as there always has been. We don't want that stuff; we want the diamonds that sparkle in the dirt, those that are using poetry to connect with audiences, to say something about the human condition, to make people think, reflect, and maybe even laugh like drains (poetry on some level is entertainment, and only an inveterate snob would say otherwise).

For some of the poets that feature in this collection, this is their first published work. For others, these poems sit alongside their other books, contributions to literary magazines etc. It doesn't matter; they're all here in one place and demanding your attention, so dive in and give them some!

Available at www.earthislandbooks.com

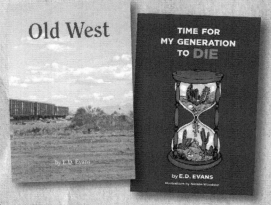

Andrea is a mess of contradictions, fan of parallel structure, and nostalgic pack rat who writes poetry about punk rock kids and takes photos of forgotten places. She believes in the beauty of the ordinary, the power of the vernacular, and the history of the abandoned. Through her work, she strives to prove that poetry can be dirty, gritty, and accessible by revealing the art in what we see, say, do, ignore, and forget every day.

Raised by rock and roll parents, she learned the importance of going to concerts and ignoring the "no trespassing" signs in her childhood. She spent her adolescence in a small town punk rock scene where she moshed, fell in love, and produced a few cut-and-paste zines, before escaping to New York City and causing a ruckus in Alphabet City. After meeting her husband in one of those Chelsea bars she has settled in Pittsburgh, is at the whim of a feisty terrier, works in tech, and still prefers Jameson neat.

After paying a few universities way too much tuition, they granted her several degrees in creative writing. When her education was complete, she started garnering some publishing credits, including a sold out run of her first book, 'Mix Tapes and Photo Albums: Memories from a small town scene'.
'Short Skirts and Whiskey Shots' picks up from where 'Mix tapes...' left off.

She is uncomfortable talking about herself, even in third person.
www.andreajanov.com

Available at www.earthislandbooks.com

OF THE

WISDOM

PUNK

BUDDHA